LIBRARY OF AWESOME ANIMALS

ATLANTIC PUFFIN

By Jennifer Wendt

Consultant: Darin Collins, DVM
Director, Animal Health Programs, Woodland Park Zoo

BEARPORT
PUBLISHING

Minneapolis, Minnesota

Credits

cover, © Arnau Soler/Shutterstock and © LouieLea/Shutterstock; 3, © JustinDutcher/Shutterstock; 4, © Kay Roxby/Alamy Stock Photo; 6, © Eric Isselee/Shutterstock; 7, © Javier Rodriguez Jimenez/iStock; 8, © Steve Biegler/Shutterstock; 8, © Diane Fetzner/Shutterstock; 9, © Jamen Percy/Shutterstock; 10, © Edward Westmacott/Shutterstock; 10, © Elena Zajchikova/Shutterstock; 10, © Picture Partners/Shutterstock; 11, © Lori Ellis/Shutterstock; 13, © sergeydolya/Shutterstock; 14, © Tosaporn/Shutterstock; 14, © Richard Whitcombe/Shutterstock; 16, © PJ photography/Shutterstock; 17, © Matthew Jellings/Alamy Stock Photo; 18, © Richardom/Alamy Stock Photo; 18, © FotoRequest/Shutterstock; 20, © Survivalphotos/Alamy Stock Photo; 21, © AGAMI Photo Agency/Alamy Stock Photo; 23, © Menno Schaefer/Shutterstock

President: Jen Jenson
Director of Product Development: Spencer Brinker
Editor: Allison Juda
Designer: Micah Edel

Library of Congress Cataloging-in-Publication Data

Names: Wendt, Jennifer, author.
Title: Atlantic puffin / Jennifer Wendt.
Description: Minneapolis, MN : Bearport Publishing Company, [2021] |
  Series: Library of awesome animals | Includes bibliographical references and index.
Identifiers: LCCN 2020008630 (print) | LCCN 2020008631 (ebook) |
  ISBN 9781647471460 (library binding) | ISBN 9781647471576 (paperback) |
  ISBN 9781647471682 (ebook)
Subjects: LCSH: Atlantic puffin—Juvenile literature.
Classification: LCC QL696.C42 W46 2021 (print) | LCC QL696.C42 (ebook) |
  DDC 598.3/3—dc23
LC record available at https://lccn.loc.gov/2020008630
LC ebook record available at https://lccn.loc.gov/2020008631

For more information, write to Bearport Publishing, 5357 Penn Avenue South, Minneapolis, MN 55419. Printed in the United States of America.

Contents

AWESOME
Atlantic Puffins!

SPLASH! An Atlantic puffin scoops up a beak full of fish. Diving deep, flying high, or waddling across land, puffins are awesome!

PUFFINS ARE SOMETIMES CALLED SEA PARROTS OR CLOWNS OF THE SEA.

Water and Sky

Puffins are **seabirds**. They can live on land and out at sea! They are great swimmers as well as great fliers. Puffins can fly up to 55 miles per hour (88 kph). To do this, they beat their wings up to 400 times a minute. **WOW!**

PUFFINS NEED A RUNNING START TO TAKE OFF FOR FLIGHT.

Black and White and Orange All Over

There are three kinds of puffins. The Atlantic puffin is the most common.

The Atlantic puffin has black and white feathers and a large, horned beak. In spring, the puffin's beak and webbed feet are bright orange. In winter, they turn a duller color. The puffin sheds the outer shell of its beak at this time.

A horned puffin

A tufted puffin

What's for Dinner?

Puffins eat small fish such as herring, sand eels, and hake. They can dive up to 200 feet (61 m) to chase their **prey**. Puffins use their wings like flippers and can stay underwater for up to one minute.

A puffin's beak has a special **hinge** that allows it to carry more than one fish in its mouth.

Herring

Sand eels

Hake

PUFFINS CAN HOLD MORE THAN 20 SMALL FISH IN THEIR BEAKS AT ONCE. AWESOME!

Stayin' Alive!

In the past, puffins almost went **extinct** in some places because humans hunted them and took their eggs. Today, pollution and changing climates are leading to a loss of puffin **habitats**.

Puffins are also **threatened** by other animals. Foxes hunt puffins, and gulls eat their eggs. Other puffin **predators** can include cats or rats when puffins live near humans.

PUFFINS STOMP THEIR FEET WHEN THEY ARE ALARMED.

A gull with
a puffin egg

13

A Wet, Watery Home

Puffins live in the northern half of the world. The Atlantic puffin lives in and near the Atlantic Ocean.

PUFFINS MAKE A LOT OF NOISE WHILE THEY ARE ON LAND, BUT THEY ARE COMPLETELY SILENT WHEN THEY ARE AT SEA.

Puffins spend most of their lives at sea. Their waterproof feathers keep them dry and warm. When puffins are not flying or swimming, they rest and sleep on the waves. They move to land during **mating season**.

Digging Deep

Puffins live in **burrows** during mating season. They dig these homes using their feet and beaks. If a puffin can't dig a burrow, it will find a hole between rocks on a sea cliff.

A puffin builds a nest in the burrow using grass and feathers.

PUFFINS KEEP THEIR NESTS CLEAN. THEY USE A DIFFERENT PART OF THEIR BURROW OR GO OUTSIDE TO POOP AND PEE.

A puffin burrow

Puffin Families

Puffins lay only one egg a year. They keep the same **mate** and use the same burrow every year. Puffin parents take turns caring for the egg. A puffin egg takes about 40 days to hatch. The chick is called a puffling. Both parents take care of the chick.

GRRR! ADULTS GROWL TO COMMUNICATE WITH THEIR FAMILIES. IT SOUNDS LIKE A CHAIN SAW.

A puffling

Leaving the Nest

A chick leaves the **colony** when it is about 40 days old. It heads to the open ocean and lives there for three to five years. It will live by itself until it is ready to mate. Then, the young puffin returns to the place where it was born to start its own family.

A GROUP OF PUFFINS IS SOMETIMES CALLED A CIRCUS.

ATLANTIC PUFFINS ARE AWESOME!
LET'S LEARN EVEN MORE ABOUT THEM.

Kind of animal: Puffins are birds. Like all birds, they are warm-blooded, are covered in feathers, and have wings.

Size: Puffins are about 10 inches (25 cm) tall. That is about the height of a gallon of milk.

Other puffins: The Atlantic puffin is one of three kinds of puffins. The other two kinds are the horned puffin and the tufted puffin.

ATLANTIC PUFFINS AROUND THE WORLD

Arctic Ocean

NORTH AMERICA

EUROPE

ASIA

Pacific Ocean

Atlantic Ocean

AFRICA

Pacific Ocean

SOUTH AMERICA

Indian Ocean

AUSTRALIA

N
W E
S

Southern Ocean

ANTARCTICA

WHERE ATLANTIC PUFFINS LIVE

Glossary

burrows holes or tunnels in the ground where animals live

colony a group of animals that shares a home

extinct when a kind of animal has died out completely

habitats places in nature where animals live

hinge a joint on which something turns or swings

mate a male or female partner

mating season the time of year when animals come together to have young

predators animals that hunt and kill other animals for food

prey animals that are hunted and eaten by other animals

seabirds birds that spend most of their lives at sea

threatened in danger

Index

Read More

Murray, Julie. *Puffins (Arctic Animals).* Minneapolis: ABDO (2014).

Oachs, Emily Rose. *Arctic Ocean (Blastoff! Readers: Discover the Oceans).* Minneapolis: Bellwether Media (2016).

Learn More Online

1. Go to **www.factsurfer.com**

2. Enter "**Atlantic Puffin**" into the search box.

3. Click on the cover of this book to see a list of websites.

About the Author

Jennifer Wendt lives in Minnesota but loves puffins and traveling to find them. She recently visited Skomer Island off the coast of Wales in the United Kingdom, where she saw thousands of puffins. **That's AWESOME!**